S0-AJF-479

AMOS OZ

How to Cure a Fanatic

Israel and Palestine:
Between Right and Right

VINTAGE BOOKS
London

Published by Vintage 2012

8 10 9

Copyright © Amos Oz 2004 updated material 2012
Foreword copyright © Nadine Gordimer 2004

Amos Oz has asserted his right under the Copyright, Designs and Patents
Act 1988 to be identified as the author of this work

First published in Great Britain by Vintage in 2004 as
Help us to Divorce.

Vintage
Random House, 20 Vauxhall Bridge Road,
London SW1V 2SA

www.vintage-books.co.uk

Addresses for companies within The Random House Group Limited can
be found at: www.randomhouse.co.uk/offices.htm

The Random House Group Limited Reg. No. 954009

A CIP catalogue record for this book is available from the British Library

ISBN 9780099572725

Penguin Random House is committed to a sustainable future for
our business, our readers and our planet. This book is made from
Forest Stewardship Council® certified paper.

Printed and bound in Great Britain by Clays Ltd, St Ives plc

Contents

Foreword by
Nadine Gordimer

Amos Oz is the voice of sanity coming out of confusion, the lying, hysterical babble of world rhetoric about current conflicts. In the brilliant clarity of 'How To Cure a Fanatic' he analyses the twisted historical roots that produce the evil flower of violence, seeded again and again. He brings us to face the nature of fanaticism, its evolution. He doesn't offer a cure-all.

But, he convinces irrefutably that the Israeli-Palestinian conflict is 'Not a religious war, not a war of cultures, not a disagreement between two traditions, but simply a real-estate dispute over whose house this is.' And he is not afraid to stake his vision and politico-moral integrity in the belief that the dispute can be resolved. 'Between Right and Right' is a down-to-ground solution for which he advocates the necessity of imagination in what human beings in certain situations basically need in order to begin to define and respect each other's space. The ironic humour with which he illuminates the vitally serious makes it all the more telling.

Publisher's Note

These essays were originally delivered as speeches in Germany in 2002. They have been edited here for the English-language edition. They are followed by a Postscript written in 2003, on the publication of the 'Geneva Accords' and which formed part of an article that appeared in a slightly different version in the *Guardian*, 17 October 2003.

BETWEEN RIGHT
AND RIGHT

Between Right And Right

Who are the good guys? That's what every well-meaning European, left-wing European, intellectual European, liberal European always wants to know, first and foremost. Who are the good guys in the film and who are the bad guys. In this respect Vietnam was easy: the Vietnamese people were the victims and the Americans were the bad guys. The same with apartheid: you could easily see that apartheid was a crime and that the struggle for equal, civil rights, for liberation and for equality and for human dignity was right. The struggle between colonialism and imperialism, on the one hand, and the victims of colonialism and imperialism, on the other hand, seems relatively simple – you can tell the good guys from the bad. When it comes to the foundations of the Israeli-Arab conflict, in particular the Israeli-Palestinian conflicts, things are not so straight-forward. And I am afraid I am not going to make things any easier for you by saying simply: these are the angels, these are the devils, you just have to support the angels and good will prevail over evil. The Israeli-Palestinian conflict is not a Wild West movie. It is not a struggle between good and evil, rather it is a tragedy in the ancient and most precise sense of the word: a clash between right and right, a clash between one very powerful, deep and convincing claim and another very different but no less convincing, no less powerful, no less humane claim.

The Palestinians are in Palestine because Palestine is the homeland and the only homeland of the Palestinian people. In the same way in which Holland is the homeland of the Dutch, or Sweden the homeland of the Swedes. The Israeli Jews are in Israel because there is no other country in the world which the Jews, as a people, as a nation, could ever call home. As individuals, yes, but not as a people, not as a nation. The Palestinians have tried, unwillingly, to live in other Arab countries. They were rejected, sometimes even humiliated and persecuted, by the so-called 'Arab family'. They were made aware in the most painful way of their 'Palestinianness', they were not wanted as Lebanese, or as Syrians, or as Egyptians, or as Iraqis. They had to learn the hard way that they are Palestinians, and that's the only country which they can hold on to. In a strange way the Jewish people, just as the Palestinian people, have had a somewhat parallel historical experience. The Jews were kicked out of Europe; my parents were virtually kicked out of Europe some seventy years ago. Just like the Palestinians were first kicked out of Palestine and then out of the Arab countries, or almost. When my father was a little boy in Poland, the streets of Europe were covered with graffiti, 'Jews, go back to Palestine', or sometimes worse: 'Dirty yids, piss off to Palestine'. When my father revisited Europe fifty years later, the walls were covered with new graffiti, 'Jews, get out of Palestine'.

People in Europe keep sending me wonderful invitations to spend a rosy weekend in a delightful resort with Palestinian partners, Palestinian colleagues, Palestinian counterparts, so that we can learn to know one another, to like one another, to drink a cup of coffee together, so that we will realise that no one has horns and tails – and the trouble will go away. This is based on a widespread sentimental European idea that every conflict is essentially no more than a misunderstanding. A little group therapy, a touch of family counselling, and everyone will live happily ever after. Well, first I have bad news for you: some conflicts are very real, they are much worse than a mere misunderstanding. And then I have some sensational news for you: there is no essential misunderstanding between Palestinian Arab and Israeli Jew. The Palestinians want the land they call Palestine. They have very strong reasons to want it. The Israeli Jews want exactly the same land for exactly the same reasons, which provides for a perfect understanding between the parties, and for a terrible tragedy. Rivers of coffee drunk together cannot extinguish the tragedy of two peoples claiming, and I think rightly claiming, the same small country as their one and only national homeland in the whole world. So, drinking coffee together is wonderful and I'm all for it, especially if it is Arabic coffee which is infinitely better than Israeli coffee. But, drinking coffee cannot do away with the trouble. What we need is not just coffee and a better understanding. What we need is a painful compromise. The word compromise has a terrible reputation in Europe. Especially among young idealists, who always regard compromise as opportunism, as something dishonest, as something sneaky and shady, as a mark of a lack of integrity. Not in my vocabulary. For me the word compromise means life. And the opposite of compromise is not idealism, not devotion; the opposite of compromise is fanaticism and death. We need a compromise. Compromise, not capitulation. A compromise means that the Palestinian people should never go down on its knees, neither should the Israeli Jewish people.

I'm going to discuss the nature of such a compromise, but right at the outset I should tell you that this compromise will be very painful. Because both peoples love the country, because both peoples, Israeli Jews and Palestinian Arabs, have equally deep, different historical and emotional roots in the country. One of the components of this tragedy, one of the aspects which has a certain irony about it, is the fact that many Israeli Jews don't recognise how deep is the Palestinian emotional connection to the land. And many Palestinians fail to recognise just how deep is the Jewish connection to the same land. However, this recognition comes in a painful way and as a painful process for both nations. It is a route paved with shattered dreams and broken illusions and injured hopes and blown-up slogans from the past on both sides.

I have worked for many years for the Israeli 'Peace Now' movement. In fact, I worked for an Israeli-Palestinian peace long before 'Peace Now' was established in 1978. Back in 1967, immediately after the Six Day War, I was among the very first and very few Israeli Jews who immediately advocated the idea of negotiating the future of the West Bank and Gaza not with Jordan or Egypt but with the Palestinian population and with the Palestinian leadership and yes, with the PLO, who at that time refused even to pronounce the word Israel. It was a strange experience in those days.

At this moment, the Israeli peace movement is injured. But let's be very clear that the Israeli peace movement is not a twin sister of pacifist movements in Europe, or in America, during the years of the

Vietnam War or more recently. We are not of the idea that if Israel pulls out of the occupied territories, everything will be solved overnight. Nor are we of the simple idea that Israel is the bad guy, certainly not the only bad guy in this story. We are pro-peace, but not necessarily pro-Palestinian. We are very critical of the Palestinian leadership. I personally am as critical of the Palestinian leadership as I am of the Israeli leadership. And I will come to that later. But the argument between ourselves and some European peace movements cuts even deeper. I have been personally on the battlefield twice in my life, for the first time as a reservist soldier with a tank unit on the Egyptian front in Sinai in 1967 and again on the Syrian front in the 1973 war. It was the most horrible experience of my whole life, and yet I'm not ashamed of fighting in those two wars. I'm not a pacifist in the sentimental sense of the word. If once again I felt that there was a real danger of my country being completely wiped off the map and my people being butchered, I would fight again, although I'm an old man. But I would only fight if I thought it was a matter of life and death, or if I thought anybody was trying to turn me or the next person into a slave. I would never fight – I would prefer to go to jail – over extra territories. I would never fight for an extra bedroom for the nation. I would never fight over holy places or holy sights. I would never fight over so-called national interests. But I would fight, and fight like the devil, for life and for freedom and for nothing else.

Now this may create a certain gap between myself and the regular European pacifist, who maintains that the ultimate evil in the world is war. In my vocabulary war is terrible, yet the ultimate evil is not war but aggression. If in 1939 the whole world except for Germany had maintained that war was the worst of all evils in the world, then Hitler would have been lord of the universe by now. So, when you recognise aggression, you have to fight against it, wherever it comes from. But only over life and freedom, not over extra territory or extra resources.

When I coined the phrase 'Make Peace Not Love', I was not, of course, preaching against making love. But I was, to some extent, trying to remove the widespread sentimental 'mish-mash' of peace and love and brotherhood and compassion and forgiveness and concession and so on, which makes people think that if only people would drop their weapons, the world would immediately become a marvellous, loving place. Personally, I happen to believe that love is a rare commodity. I think a human being, at least in my experience, can love ten people. If he's very generous he can love twenty people. A lucky human being, a very lucky human being, may even be loved by ten people. If he's exceedingly lucky, he may be loved by twenty people. If someone says to me that she loves Latin America, or he loves the Third World, or they love humanity, it is too thin to be meaningful. As a popular song lamented, many years ago, 'there's just not enough love to go round'. I don't think love is the virtue by which we solve international problems. We need other virtues. We need a sense of justice, but we also need common sense, we need imagination, a deep ability to imagine the other, sometimes to put ourselves in the skin of the other. We need the rational ability to compromise and sometimes to make sacrifices and concessions, but we don't need to commit suicide for the sake of peace. 'I'll kill myself so that you will be happy.' Or, 'I want you to kill yourself because that will make me happy.' And those two attitudes are not dissimilar; they are closer than you think.

In my view, the opposite of war is not love, and the opposite of war is not compassion, and the opposite of war is not generosity or brotherhood, or forgiveness. No, the opposite of war is peace. Nations need to live in peace. If I see in my lifetime the State of Israel and the State of Palestine, living next door to each other as decent neighbours without oppression, without exploitation, without bloodshed, without terror, without violence, I will be sated even if love does not prevail. And, as the poet Robert Frost reminded us, 'Good fences makes good neighbors.'

One of the things which makes this conflict particularly hard is the fact that the Israeli-Palestinian, the Israeli-Arab conflict, is essentially a conflict between two victims. Two victims of the same oppressor. Europe, which colonised the Arab world, exploited it, humiliated it, trampled upon its culture, controlled it and used it as an imperialistic playground, is the same Europe which discriminated against the Jews, persecuted them, harassed them, and finally, mass-murdered them in an unprecedented crime of genocide. Now, you would have thought that two victims immediately

develop between themselves a sense of
solidarity – as, for instance, in the poetry
of Bertolt Brecht. But in real life, some
of the worst conflicts are precisely the
conflicts between two victims of the same
oppressor. Two children of the same cruel
parent do not necessarily love one
another. Very often they see in each other
the exact image of the cruel parent.

And this is precisely the case not just
between Israeli and Palestinian but between
Jew and Arab. Each one of the parties looks
at the other and sees in the other the image
of their past oppressors. In much contem-
porary Arabic literature, though not in all
of it (and I have to make a reservation here:
I can read Arabic literature only in translation, as unfortunately I do not read
Arabic) the Jew, especially the Israeli Jew,
is often pictured as an extension of the

white, sophisticated, tyrannising, colonis-
ing, cruel, heartless Europe of the past.
These are the colonialists, who came to the
Middle East once again, this time disguised
as Zionists, but they came to tyrannise, to
colonise and to exploit. These are the same
people – we know them. Very often Arabs,
even some sensitive Arab writers, fail to see
us as what we, Israeli Jews, really are – a
bunch of half-hysterical refugees and
survivors, haunted by dreadful nightmares,
traumatised not only by Europe but also
by the way we were treated in Arabic and
Islamic countries. Half the population of
Israel are people who were kicked out of
Arabic and Islamic countries. Israel is
indeed one large Jewish refugee camp. Half
of us are actually Jewish refugees from
Arab countries, but Arabs don't see us this
way; they see us as an extension of

colonialism. By the same token we, Israeli Jews, don't see the Arabs, particularly the Palestinians, as what they are: victims of centuries of oppression, exploitation, colonialism and humiliation. No, we see them as pogrom-makers and Nazis, who just wrapped themselves in koffias and grew moustaches and got sun-tanned, but are in the same old game of cutting the throats of the Jews for fun. In short, they are our past oppressors all over again. In this respect there is a deep ignorance on both sides: not political ignorance about the purposes and the goals, but about the backgrounds, about the deep traumas of the two victims.

I've been very critical of the Palestinian national movement for many years. Some of the reasons are historical, some of the reasons are not. But mostly I have been

critical of the Palestinian national movement for failing to realise how genuine the
Jewish connection to the land of Israel is.
Failing to realise that modern Israel is not
a product of a colonialist enterprise, or at
least failing to tell it to their people. I should
tell you immediately that I'm equally critical of generations of Israeli Zionists, who
failed to imagine that there is a Palestinian
people, a real people, with real and legitimate rights. So both leaderships past and,
yes, present are guilty of either not understanding the tragedy, or at least not telling
their people.

Well, I don't believe in a sudden burst
of mutual love between Israel and Palestine.
I don't expect that, once some miraculous
formula is found, the two antagonists will
suddenly hug one another in tears in a
Dostoyevskian scene of long-lost brothers

reconciled – 'O my brother, will you ever forgive me, how could I be so terrible, take the land, who cares about the land, just give me your love.' Unfortunately, I don't expect anything like this. I don't expect a honeymoon either. If anything, I expect a fair and just divorce between Israel and Palestine. And divorces are never happy, even when they are more or less just. They still hurt, they are painful. Especially this particular divorce which is going to be a very peculiar divorce, because the two divorcing parties are definitely staying in the same apartment. No one is moving out. And the apartment being very small, it will be necessary to decide who gets bedroom A and who gets bedroom B and how about the living room; and the apartment being so small, some special arrangement has to be made about the bathroom and the kitchen. Very inconvenient. But better than the kind of living hell which everyone is going through now in that beloved country. A country where Palestinian men, women and children are daily oppressed, haunted, humiliated, deprived by the cruel Israeli military government. A country where Israeli people are daily terrorised by ruthless indiscriminate terrorist attacks on civilians, men, women, children, schoolboys, teenagers, shoppers in a mall. Anything is preferable to this! Especially, a fair divorce. And eventually perhaps, after we have conducted this painful fair divorce by creating two states, divided roughly according to demographic realities – and I'm not going to try to draw a map here, but I can tell you, in a nutshell, that essentially the lines should be similar to the pre-1967 lines, with some mutually agreed

modifications and some special arrange-
ments for the disputed holy places in
Jerusalem – once this divorce is conducted and a partition is created, I
believe Israelis and Palestinians will be
quick to hop over the partition for a cup
of coffee together.

That will be the time for coffee
together. Moreover, I predict that, shortly
after the partition solution is implemented, we shall be in a position to cook
our meals together in the little kitchen, by
which I mean shared economy. Perhaps a
common Middle Eastern market. Perhaps
a Middle Eastern currency. Of one thing
I can assure Europeans: our conflict in
the Middle East is indeed painful and
bloody and cruel and stupid, but it's not
going to take us a thousand years to
produce our equivalent of the Euro

currency of the Middle East; we will be faster than you were, and shed less blood than you did. So, before you people look down at us, Jewish idiots, Arab idiots, cruel people, fanatical people, extremist people, violent people, be a little more careful in wagging your fingers at all of us. Our bloody history is going to be shorter than your bloody history. I know it's very dangerous to make prophecies when you come from my part of the world. There is a lot of competition in the prophecy business over there. But, I can stick my neck out and predict that we are not going to spend hundreds of years butchering one another in the time-honoured European tradition. We will be quicker than that. How much quicker? I wish I could answer you. I never under-estimate the short-sightedness and the stupidity of political leaderships on both sides. But it will happen.

Moreover, the crucial first step ought to be, must be, a two-state solution. Israel must go back to what has been the initial Israeli proposition since 1948 and even before '48, from the beginning: recognition for recognition, statehood for statehood, independence for independence, security for security. Good neighbourliness for good neighbourliness, respect for respect. The Palestinian leadership for its part must turn to its own people and say at last, loud and clear, something that it has never succeeded in pronouncing, namely that Israel is not an accident of history, that Israel is not an intrusion, that Israel happens to be the homeland of the Israeli Jews, no matter how painful this is for the Palestinians. Just as we Israeli Jews have to say loud and clear that Palestine is the homeland of the Palestinian people, very inconvenient as this may seem to us.

The worst part of the Israeli-Arab, the Israeli-Palestinian conflict is not now, it's in those many years, many decades, when the two parties could not even pronounce each other's names. When Palestinians and other Arabs had a real difficulty pronouncing the dirty word Israel. They used to call it the 'Zionist entity', the 'artificial creature', the 'intrusion', the 'infection', 'Al Daula al-Maz'ouma' – the 'artificial state', or the artificial being. For a very long time many Arabs and most Palestinians maintained that Israel was some kind of mobile exhibition. If they protested loudly enough the world would take Israel and transplant it elsewhere, maybe in Australia or some other faraway place. They treated Israel like a nightmare, a '*koshmar*', if they rubbed their eyes hard enough Israel would go away. They treated Israel like a passing infection, if they scratched it and scratched it, it would go somehow. And indeed they tried a couple of times, or actually several times, to undo Israel by military force. They failed and became very frustrated over this failure. But in the same years the Israelis were no better. The Israelis, for their part, failed even to pronounce the explicit words 'Palestinian people'. We used to resort to euphemisms, such as 'the locals' or 'the Arab inhabitants of the land'. We were more pan-Arabic than the Naser regime in Egypt, because if you happen to be pan-Arabic then there is no Palestinian problem. The Arab world is huge. For many years we Israelis blinded ourselves to the fact that the Palestinian people could not find a home even in Arab countries. We did not want to see and hear this.

Those times are past. The two peoples now ought each to realise that the other is real; and most people on both sides now know that the other is not going to go away. Are they happy about it? Not at all. Is this a cheerful moment? Not at all. It's a painful moment. It's more like, for both sides, waking up in a hospital, after an anaesthetic slumber and finding out that you have been amputated. And this, let me tell you, is a bad hospital and the doctors are not wonderful, and the two families outside the operating theatre are cursing each other and cursing the doctors. This is the picture of the Middle East right now. But everybody at least knows, that surgery is unavoidable, everybody now knows, that the country will have to be partitioned somehow into two national states. One country which will be predominantly, not exclusively, but predominantly Jewish, because the Jews have a right to be a majority in one small land, which, after Israel's withdrawal, will probably be one-third the size of a British county. But this will be a place, which will be recognised by Israeli Jews, by the whole world, even by our neighbours, as our national home. But the price for this must be that the Palestinian people will have the same right. They will have a homeland, one which will be even smaller than Israel, but it will be home, their home.

But more urgent than the question of boundaries, more urgent than the question of the disputed holy places, more urgent than any other question, is the question of what to do about the tragedy of the Palestinian refugees of 1948. Those people who lost their homes, and who in some cases lost their homeland, lost everything, during Israel's War of Independence in 1948. There is a deep disagreement on where to put the blame, or most of the blame, for this tragedy. You will find some modern Israeli historians who put the blame on Israel. I suppose in a few years eventually, and I hope to live to see this day, you will find some modern Arab historians who will put the blame on the Arab governments of that time. But regardless of who, finally, takes how much of the blame, this issue is urgent and immediate. Every single Palestinian refugee, who is homeless, and jobless, and country-less should be provided with a home and a job and a passport. Israel cannot admit those people, at least not in vast numbers. If it does, it will no longer be Israel. Yet Israel should be part of the solution. Israel should also admit part of the responsibility for their tragedy. What percentage of the responsibility is a very academic question and probably a very subjective question. But part of the responsibility lies with Israel. The other part lies with the Palestinian leadership of 1947 and with the Arab governments of '48. Israel has to help to resettle the refugees in future Palestine, that is in the West Bank and Gaza, or elsewhere. Of course, Israel is perfectly within its rights to bring up the subject of one million Jewish refugees from Arab countries, who also lost their homes and their properties following the 1948 war. These Jews don't want to go back to the Arab countries. But they, too, have left everything behind them – in Iraq, in Syria, in Yemen, in Egypt, in North Africa, in Iran, in Lebanon, as they were virtually pushed out of these countries, sometimes even forced out. So, all of this ought to be taken care of.

If I were Prime Minister of Israel I would not sign any peace agreement which did not resolve the issues of the Palestinian refugees, by re-settling them in the state of Palestine. Because any resolution which doesn't take care of the issue of the refugees is a time-bomb. Not only for moral reasons, even for selfish reasons of Israel's security, this human and national problem must be resolved within the framework of the immediate peace process. Fortunately we are not speaking of the whole of Africa, or India. We are talking about a few hundred thousand homes and jobs. Not every

Palestinian refugee is homeless and country-less right now. But those who are homeless and country-less and are rotting in inhuman conditions in refugee camps – their problem is my problem. If there is no solution for these people, Israel will have no peace and quiet even if it has an agreement with its neighbour.

I want to propose the first joint project that Israeli Jews and Palestinian Arabs will have to initiate, as soon as the divorce between them is conducted and the two-state solution is implemented. The first joint project, for which we should take no foreign help at all and for which the two nations should make an equal investment, dollar for dollar, ought to be a shared monument to our past stupidities, to our past idiocies. Because everybody knows that when the peace treaty is finally implemented one day, the Palestinian people are going to get a lot less than they could have got fifty-five years ago, five wars ago, one hundred and fifty thousand dead ago, our dead and their dead. If only the Palestinian leadership in 1947–48 had been less fanatic and one-sided and less uncompromising, if only it had accepted the UN partition resolution of November 1947. But the Israeli leadership will also have to contribute to that monument to stupidity, because we Israelis could have got ourselves a much better deal, a much more convincing deal, if we had been less arrogant, less power-intoxicated, less self-ish and less unimaginative after our military victory in 1967.

So, the two nations will have a lot of soul searching to do, about their past mutual stupidities. However, the good news is that the cognitive block is gone. If you passed a referendum now, or a public-opinion survey between the Mediterranean and the River Jordan, asking every single individual regardless of religion, or status, or politics, or passport or lack of passport – every individual – not what would you regard as a just solution, not what would you like to see, but what do you actually think is going to happen at the end of the day, I guess about eighty per cent would say: 'a partition and a two-state solution'. Some people would immediately add: 'and this will be the end of everything, and this will be a terrible injustice!' On both sides people would say that. But, at least most of the people know now. The good news is that, I think, both the Jewish Israeli people and the Palestinian Arab people are ahead of their leaders, for the first time in a hundred years. When finally a visionary leader stands up on both sides and says: 'This is it! This is it! Biblical dreams – you may all go on dreaming them, pre-'47 dreams, post-'67 dreams, these fantasies or those fantasies, you may go on dreaming, there is no censorship on fantasies. But the reality is roughly the 1967 lines.' Give or take an inch here or there, by mutual agreement. And some open-ended formula for the disputed holy places, because only an open-ended arrangement can work there. In that moment, when the leaders on both sides are ready to say this, they will find the two peoples sadly ready for it. Not happily, but ready for it. More ready than ever before. Ready in the hard way, ready through pain and bloodshed, but ready.

I want to make one last point. What can you do? What can public-opinion makers do? What can Europeans do? What can the outside world do, apart from shaking their heads and saying, 'How terrible!'? Well, there are two things, perhaps three. One, public-opinion makers across Europe are in the miserable habit of wagging their index finger, like an old-fashioned Victorian headmistress, at this side, or at that side: 'Aren't you ashamed of yourselves?' Too often I find in the papers in various European countries either terrible things about Israel or terrible things about the Arabs and about Islam. Simple-minded things, narrow-minded things, self-righteous things. I'm no longer a European in any sense, except through the pain of my parents and my ancestors, who left for ever in my genes a sense of unrequited love

for Europe. But if I were a European, I'd
be careful not to wag my finger at anyone
at all. Instead of wagging your finger, call-
ing the Israelis this name or the Palestinians
that name, I would do anything I could to
help both sides, because both are on the
verge of making the most painful decision
of their histories. The Israelis, by relinquish-
ing the occupied territories, by removing
most of the settlements, will have not only
to retract their own self-image and face a
serious internal clash and rift. They will be
taking very serious security risks, not from
Palestine, but from future extremist Arabic
powers who may, one day, use Palestinian
territory to launch an attack on Israel,
which after the withdrawal will be only
twelve kilometres wide right at the hip. It
means that the boundary of the future
Palestinian state will start about seven

kilometres from our one and only international airport. Palestine will be within twenty kilometres of about half the Israeli Jewish population. Jerusalem will be on the border. This is not an easy decision for the Israelis to make and yet they have to make it. The Palestinians, on their side, will have to sacrifice parts which used to be their own before 1948, and this is going to hurt. Goodbye Haifa, goodbye Jaffa, goodbye Beer Sheva, and many other towns and villages, which used to be Arabic and are no longer and will never again be part of Palestine. This is going to hurt like hell. So, if you have an ounce of help or sympathy to offer, now is the time to extend it to the two patients. You no longer have to choose between being pro-Israel or pro-Palestine. You have to be pro-peace.

HOW TO CURE
A FANATIC

How To Cure A Fanatic

So, how do you cure a fanatic? To chase a bunch of fanatics through the mountains of Afghanistan is one thing. To struggle against fanaticism is another one. I'm afraid I don't have any particular ideas on how to catch the fanatics in the mountains, but I do have one or two thoughts about the nature of fanaticism and about the ways, if not to cure it, then at least to contain it. The attack on America on September 11th was not simply about poverty versus wealth. Poverty versus wealth is one of the world's most horrible problems, but we will misdiagnose such terrorist attacks if we simply think that this was an attack from the poor on the rich. It is not just about the 'haves' and the 'have-nots'. If the case were as simple as that, you would rather expect the attack to come from Africa, the poorest, and perhaps to be launched against Saudi Arabia and the Gulf, the oil-producing states, the richest. No, this is a battle between fanatics, who believe that the end, any end, justifies the means, and the rest of us, who believe that life is an end, not a meaning. It is a struggle between those who think that justice, whatever they would mean by the word, is more important than life, on the one hand, and those of us who think that life takes priority over many other values, convictions or faiths. The present crisis in the world, in the Middle East, in Israel/Palestine, is not about the values of Islam. It is not about the mentality of the Arabs, as some racists claim, not at all. It is about the ancient struggle between fanaticism and pragmatism. Between fanaticism and pluralism. Between fanaticism and tolerance. September 11th was not even about the question of whether America is good or bad, whether capitalism is ugly or evident, whether globalisation should stop or not. This was about the typical fanatic claim: if I think something is bad, I kill it along with its neighbours.

Fanaticism is older than Islam, older than Christianity, older than Judaism, older than any state or any government, or political system, older than any ideology or faith in the world. Fanaticism is unfortunately an ever-present component of human nature; an evil gene, if you like. People who blow up abortion clinics in America, people who burn mosques and synagogues in Europe, differ from Bin Laden only in the scale but not in the nature of their crimes. Of course, September 11th evoked sadness, anger, disbelief, shock, melancholy, disorientation and, yes, some racist responses – anti-Arab and anti-Muslim racist responses everywhere. Who would have thought that the twentieth century would be immediately followed by the eleventh century?

My own childhood in Jerusalem rendered me an expert in comparative fanaticism. Jerusalem of my childhood, back in the 1940s, was full of self-proclaimed prophets, Redeemers and Messiahs. Even today, every other Jerusalemite has his or her personal formula for instant salvation. Everyone says they came to Jerusalem, and I'm quoting a famous line from an old song, they came to Jerusalem to build it and to be built by it. In fact, some of them, Jews, Christians and Muslims, socialists, anarchists, world-reformers, actually came to Jerusalem not so much to build it, not so much to be built by it, but rather to get crucified, or to crucify others, or both. There is an established mental disorder, a recognised mental illness known as 'the Jerusalem syndrome': People come to Jerusalem, they inhale the wonderful lucid mountain air, and then they suddenly up and set fire to a mosque or to a church or to a synagogue. Or else, they simply take off their clothes, climb on the rock and start prophesying. No one ever listens. Even today, even in today's Jerusalem, every line for a bus is likely to spark and turn into a fiery street seminar, with total strangers arguing about politics, morality, strategy, history, identity, religion and the real purpose of God. Participants in such street seminars, while arguing about politics and theology, good and evil, try nevertheless to elbow their way to the front of the line. Everyone screams, no one ever listens. Except for me. I listen sometimes, that's how I earn my living.

Yet, I confess, that as a child in Jerusalem I was myself a brainwashed little fanatic all the way. Self-righteous, chauvinistic, deaf and blind to any

narrative that differed from the powerful Jewish, Zionist narrative of the time.
I was a stone-throwing kid, a Jewish
Intifada kid. In fact, the first words I
ever learned to say in English except for
'yes' and 'no', were the words: 'British,
go home!', which is what we Jewish kids
used to shout as we were throwing stones
at the British patrols in Jerusalem.
Talking about ironies of history – in my
1995 novel, *Panther in the Basement*, I
described how the boy, Proffy by name,
or by nickname, loses his fanaticism, he
loses his chauvinism, up to a point at
least, and he is changed almost in the
space of two weeks through a sense of
relativism, through the shock of
relativism. He happens to befriend,
secretly, an enemy, namely a very sweet,
ineffectual British police sergeant. And

they meet secretly, the boy and the British sergeant, and they teach each other English and Hebrew. And the boy discovers that women have no horns and no tail, which is almost as shocking a revelation for this boy as the discovery that British or Arabs have no horns and no tails. So, in a sense, the boy develops a sense of ambivalence, a capacity for abandoning his black and white views, but, of course, the price he pays is that by the end of this short novel he is no longer a child, he is a little grown-up, he is a small adult. Much of the joy and the fascination and the zeal and the simpleness of life has gone away. And besides, he is getting to be nicknamed, to be called a traitor by his old friends. I am going to take the liberty of quoting from the first page and a half of

Panther in the Basement[*], because I
think this is as close to myself, on the
issue of fanaticism, as I could ever get.

I have been called a traitor many
times in my life. The first time was
when I was twelve and a quarter
and I lived in a neighbourhood at
the edge of Jerusalem. It was during
the summer holidays, less than a
year before the British left the country and the state of Israel was born
out of the midst of war.

One morning these words
appeared on the wall of our house,
painted in thick black letters, just
under the kitchen window: PROFI

[*] Translation by Nicholas de Lange (Vintage, London,
1997)

BOGED SHAFEL. 'Proffy is a low-down traitor.' The word *shafel*, 'low-down', raised a question that still interests me now, as I sit and write this story. Is it possible for a traitor not to be low-down? If not, why did Chita Reznik (I recognized his writing) bother to add the word 'low-down'? And if it is, under what circumstances is treachery not low-down?

I had had the nickname Proffy, attached to me ever since I was so high. It was short for Professor, which they called me because of my obsession with checking words. (I still love words. I like collecting, arranging, shuffling, reversing, combining them. Rather the way people who love money so are the same with coins and banknotes and people who love cards do with cards.)

My father saw the writing under the kitchen window when he went out to get the newspaper at half past six that morning. Over breakfast, while he was spreading raspberry jam on the slice of black bread, he suddenly plunged the knife into the jam jar, almost up to the handle, and said in his deliberate way:

'What a pleasant surprise. And what has His Lordship been up to now that we should deserve this honour?' My mother said:

'Don't get at him first thing in the morning, it's bad enough that he's always being got at by other children.'

Father was dressed in khaki, like most men in our neighbourhood in those days. He had the gestures and voice of a man who is definitely in the right. Dredging up a sticky mass of raspberry from the bottom of the jar and spreading an equal amount on both halves of the slice of bread, he said:

'The fact is that almost everyone nowadays uses the word "traitor" too freely. But what is a traitor? Yes indeed. A man without honour. A man who secretly, behind your back, for the sake of some questionable advantage, helps the enemy to work against his people. Or to harm his family and friends. He is more despicable than a murderer. Finish your egg, please. I read in the paper that people are dying of hunger in Asia.'

Later on in this novel, the reader may find out that the mother was totally wrong: Only he who loves might become a traitor. Treason is not the opposite to love, it is one of its many options. Traitor, I think, is the one who changes in the eyes of those who cannot change and would not change and hate change and cannot conceive of change, except that they always want to change you. In other words, traitor, in the eyes of the fanatic, is anyone who changes. And that's a tough choice, the choice between becoming a fanatic or becoming a traitor. In a sense, not to be a fanatic means to be, to some extent and in some way, a traitor in the eyes of the fanatic. I have made my choice, as *Panther in the Basement* will tell you.

I have called myself an expert of comparative fanaticism. This is no joke.

If you ever hear of a school or university starting a department of comparative fanaticism, I am hereby applying for a teaching post. As a former Jerusalemite, as a recovered fanatic, I feel I'm fully qualified for that job. Perhaps it is time that every school, every university conducts at least a couple of courses in comparative fanaticism, because it is everywhere. I don't mean just the obvious manifestations of fundamentalism and zealotry. I don't refer just to those obvious fanatics, the ones we see on television, in places where hysterical crowds wave their fists against the cameras while screaming slogans in languages we don't understand. No, fanaticism is almost everywhere, and its quieter, more civilised forms are present all around us and perhaps inside ourselves as well. Do I know the anti-smokers who will burn you alive for lighting a cigarette near them! Do I know the vegetarians who will eat you alive for eating meat! Do I know the pacifists, some of my colleagues in the Israeli Peace Movement, who are willing to shoot me right through the head just because I advocate a slightly different strategy on how to make peace with the Palestinians. So, I'm not saying, of course, that anyone who raises his or her voice against anything is a fanatic. I'm certainly not suggesting that anyone who has strong opinions is a fanatic. I'm saying that the seed of fanaticism always lies in uncompromising righteousness, the plague of many centuries. Of course, there are degrees of evil. A militant environmentalist may be uncompromisingly righteous, but he or she will cause very little harm compared, say, to an ethnic cleanser or a terrorist. Yet all fanatics have a special attraction, a special taste for kitsch. Very often, the fanatic can only count up to one; two is too big a figure for him or for her. At the same time you will find that very often fanatics are hopelessly sentimental: they often prefer feeling to thinking and have a particular fascination with their own death. They despise this world and feel eager to trade it for 'heaven'. Their heaven, however, is usually conceived like the everlasting happiness in the conclusion of bad movies.

Let me digress into a story, I'm a notorious digresser, I always digress. A dear friend and colleague of mine, the wonderful Israeli novelist Sammy Michael, had once the experience, that some of us writers have from time to time, of a very long inter-city car drive with a chauffeur who was giving him the usual lecture on how urgent it is for us Jews to kill all the Arabs. And Sammy listened to him and rather than scream, 'What a terrible man you are. Are you a Nazi, are you a fascist?' he decided to deal with it differently. He asked the chauffeur: 'And who do you think should kill all the Arabs?' The chauffeur said: 'What do you mean? Us! The Israeli Jews! We must! There is no choice, just look at what they are doing to us every day!' 'But who exactly do you think should carry our the job? The police? Or the army? Or maybe the fire brigade? Or the medical teams? Who should do the job?' The chauffeur scratched his head and said: 'I think it should be fairly divided between every one of us, every one of us should kill some of them.' Sammy Michael, still playing the game, said: 'OK, suppose you are allocated a certain residential block in your home town of Haifa and you knock on every door, or ring the door-bell asking: "Excuse me, sir, or excuse me, madam, do you happen to be an Arab?" and if the answer is yes, you shoot them. Then you finish your block and are about to go home, but just as you turn to go home,' Sammy said to the chauffeur, 'you hear somewhere on the fourth floor in your block a baby crying. Would you go back and shoot this baby? Yes or no?' There was a moment of quiet and then the chauffeur said to Sammy Michael: 'You know, you are a very cruel man.' Now, this is a significant story because there is something in the nature of the fanatic which essentially is very sentimental and at the same time lacks imagination. And this sometimes gives me hope, albeit a very limited hope, that injecting some imagination into people may help cause the fanatic to feel uneasy. This is not a quick remedy, this is not a quick cure, but it may help.

Conformity and uniformity, the urge to belong and the desire to make everyone else belong, may well be the most widely spread yet not the most dangerous forms of fanaticism. Remember the moment in that wonderful film, Monty Python's *Life of Brian*, when Brian says to the crowd of his would-be disciples: 'You are all individuals!', and the crowd shouts back: 'We are all individuals!' except one of them who says sheepishly, in a small voice: 'I'm not,' but everyone angrily hushes him. Indeed, having said that conformity and uniformity are mild but widespread forms of fanaticism, I have to add that very often the cult of personality, the idealisation of political or religious leaders, the worship of glamorous individuals, may well be another widespread form of fanaticism. The twentieth century seems to have excelled in both. Totalitarian regimes, deadly ideologies, aggressive chauvinism, violent forms of religious fundamentalism on the one hand and the universal idolisation of a Madonna or a Maradona on the other. Perhaps the worst aspect of globalisation is the infantilisation of humankind: 'the global kindergarten', full of toys and gadgets, candies and lollipops. Up to the mid-nineteenth century, give or take a few years – it varies from one country to another, from one continent to another – but roughly, up to somewhere in the nineteenth century, most people in most parts of the world had at least three basic certainties: where I will spend my life, what I will do for a living and what will happen to me after I die. Almost everyone in the world, just a hundred and fifty years ago or so, knew that they were going to spend their lives right where they were born or somewhere nearby, perhaps in the next village. Everyone knew they would do for a living what their parents did for their living or something very similar. And everyone knew that, if they behaved themselves they would be transformed to a better world after they died. The twentieth century has eroded, often destroyed, these and other certainties. The loss of those elemental certainties may have provided for the most heavily ideological half-century, followed by the most fiercely selfish, hedonistic, gadget-orientated half-century. For the ideological movements of the first half of the last century the mantra used to be 'tomorrow will be a better day – let's make sacrifices today'; let's even impose sacrifices on other people today, so that our children will inherit a paradise in the future. Somewhere around the middle of that century, this notion was replaced by the notion of instant happiness, not just the famous right to strive for happiness, but the actual widespread illusion that happiness is displayed on the shelves and that all you have to do is simply make yourself rich enough to afford happiness with your wallet. The notion of 'happily ever after', the illusion of lasting happiness, is actually an oxymoron. Either plateau or climax. Everlasting happiness is no happiness, just like an everlasting orgasm is no orgasm at all.

The essence of fanaticism lies in the desire to force other people to change. The common inclination to improve your neighbour, or to mend your spouse, or to engineer your child, or to straighten up your brother, rather than let them be. The fanatic is a most unselfish creature. The fanatic is a great altruist. Often the fanatic is more interested in you than in himself. He wants to save your soul, he wants to redeem you, he wants to liberate you from sin, from error, from smoking, from your faith or from your faithlessness, he wants to improve your eating habits, or to cure you from your drinking or voting habits. The fanatic cares a great deal for you, he is always either falling on your neck because he truly loves you or else he is at your throat in case you prove to be unredeemable. And, in any case, topographically speaking, falling on your neck and being at your throat are almost the same gesture. One way or another, the fanatic is more interested in you than in himself, for the very simple reason that the fanatic has a very little self or no self at all. Mister Bin Laden and his ilk do not just hate the West. It's not that simple. Rather, I think they want to save your souls, they want to liberate you, us, from our awful values, from materialism, from pluralism, from democracy, from freedom of speech, from women's liberation . . . All these, the Islamic fundamentalists maintain – are very, very bad for your health. Bin Laden's immediate target may have been New York, or Madrid, but his goal was to turn moderate, pragmatic Muslims into 'true' believers, into his kind of Muslims. Islam, in Bin Laden's view was weakened by 'American values', and to defend Islam, you must not just hit the West and hit it hard, you must eventually convert the West. Peace will prevail only when the world is converted not to Islam, but to the most fundamentalist and fierce and rigid form of Islam. It will be good for you. Bin Laden essentially loves you: by his way of thinking September 11th was a labour of love. He did it for your own good, he wants to change you, he wants to redeem you.

Very often, these things begin in the family. Fanaticism begins at home. It begins precisely with the very common urge to change a beloved kin for his or her own good. It begins with the urge to sacrifice oneself for the sake of a dearly beloved neighbour, it begins with the urge to tell a child of yours, 'You must become like me not like your mother,' or 'You must become like me not like your father,' or, 'Please, become something very different from both your parents.' Or, among married couples, 'You have to change, you have to see things my way or else this marriage is not going to work.' Very often it begins with the urge to live your life through someone else's life. To give yourself up in order to facilitate the next person's fulfilment or the next generation's well being. Self-sacrifice very often involves inflicting dreadful feelings of guilt upon the beneficiary, thus manipulating, even controlling, him or her. If I had to choose between the two stereotypical mothers in the famous Jewish joke – the mother who says to her kid, 'Finish your breakfast or I'll kill you,' or the one who says, 'Finish your breakfast or I'll kill myself,' – I would probably choose the lesser of two evils. That is, rather not finish my breakfast and die, than not finish my breakfast and be guilt-ridden for the rest of my life.

Let us turn now to the gloomy role of fanatics and fanaticism in the conflict between Israel and Palestine, Israel and much of the Arab world. The Israeli-Palestinian clash is essentially not a civil war between two segments of the same population, or the same people, or the same culture. It is not an internal but an international conflict. Which is fortunate, as international conflicts are easier to resolve than internal conflicts, religious wars, class wars, value wars. I said easier, I did not say easy. Essentially the battle between Israeli Jews and Palestinian Arabs is not a religious war, although the fanatics on both sides are trying very hard to turn it into a religious war. It is essentially no more than a territorial conflict over the painful question of 'whose land?'. It is a conflict between right and right, between two very powerful, very convincing claims over the same small country. Not a religious war, not a war of cultures, not a disagreement between two traditions, but simply a real-estate dispute over whose house this is. And I believe this can be resolved.

In a small way, in a cautious way, I do believe that imagination may serve as a partial and limited immunity to fanaticism. I believe that a person who can imagine what his or her ideas imply when it comes to the crying baby on the fourth floor, such a person may become a less complete fanatic, which is a slight improvement. I wish I could tell you at this point that literature is the answer, because literature contains an antidote to fanaticism by injecting imagination into its readers. I wish I could simply prescribe: read literature and you will be cured of your fanaticism. Unfortunately, it's not that simple. Unfortunately, many poems, many stories and dramas throughout history have been used to inflate hatred and to inflate nationalistic self-righteousness. Yet, there are certain works of literature which, I believe can help up to a point. They cannot work miracles, but they can help. Shakespeare can help a great deal. Every extremism, every uncompromising crusade, every form of fanaticism in Shakespeare ends up either in a tragedy or in a comedy. The fanatic is never happier or more satisfied in the end; either he is dead or he becomes a

joke. This is a good innoculation. And
Gogol can help, too: Gogol makes his
readers grotesquely aware of how little we
know, even when we are convinced that
we are one hundred per cent right. Gogol
teaches us that your nose may become a
terrible enemy, may even become a fanatic
enemy, and you may find yourself fanat-
ically chasing your own nose. Not a bad
lesson in itself. Kafka is a good educator
in this respect, although I am sure he
never meant to be used as an education
against fanaticism. Kafka shows us that
there is darkness and enigma and mock-
ery even when we think we have done
nothing wrong at all. That helps. (And
had we but world enough and time, I
would go on at length about Kafka and
Gogol and the connection, the subtle
connection, I see between these two, but

that's for another occasion.) And William Faulkner can help. The Israeli poet Yehuda Amichai expresses all of this better that I could ever hope to express it, when he says 'Where we are right no flowers can grow.' It's a very useful line. So, to some extent, some works of literature can help, but not all of them.

And if you promise to take what I'm about to say with a big pinch of salt, I can tell you that, in principle at least, I think I have invented the remedy for fanaticism. A sense of humour is a great cure. I have never once in my life seen a fanatic with a sense of humour, nor have I ever seen a person with a sense of humour becoming a fanatic, unless he or she has lost that sense of humour. Fanatics are often sarcastic. Some of them have a very pointed sense of sarcasm, but no humour. Humour contains the ability to laugh at ourselves. Humour is relativism, humour is the ability to see yourself as others may see you, humour is the capacity to realise that no matter how righteous you are and how terribly wronged against you have been, there is a certain side to life that is always a bit funny. The more right you are, the more funny you become. And, for that matter, you can be a righteous Israeli or a righteous Palestinian or a righteous anything, but, as long as you have a sense of humour, you might be partially immune to fanaticism.

If I could only compress a sense of humour into capsules and persuade entire populations to swallow my humour pills, thus immunising everybody against fanaticism, I might qualify one day for the Nobel Prize in medicine, not in literature.

But just listen to me! The very idea of compressing sense of humour into capsules, the very idea of making other people swallow my humour pills for their own good, thus curing them of their trouble, is already slightly contaminated with fanaticism. Be very careful, fanaticism is extremely catching, more contagious than any virus. You might easily contract fanaticism even as you are trying to defeat it or combat it. You have only to read a newspaper, or watch the television news, and you can see how easily people may become anti-fanatic fanatics, anti-fundamentalist zealots, anti-Jihad crusaders. Eventually, if we cannot defeat fanaticism, perhaps we can at least contain it a little bit. As I have said, the ability to laugh at ourselves is a partial cure, the ability to see ourselves as others see us is another medicine. The ability to exist within open-ended situations, even to learn how to enjoy open-ended situations, to learn to enjoy diversity, may also help. I am not preaching a complete moral relativism, certainly not. I am trying to enhance the need to imagine each other. On every level, on the most everyday level, just imagine each other. Imagine each other when we quarrel, imagine each other when we complain, imagine each other precisely at the very moment when we feel that we are one hundred per cent right. Even when you are one hundred per cent right and the other is one hundred per cent wrong, it's still useful to imagine this other. In fact, we do it all the time. My last novel, *The Same Sea*, is about a bunch of six or seven people who are scattered all over the globe and have between them almost mystical communion. They sense each other, they communicate with each other all the time, in telepathic ways, although they are scattered in the four corners of the earth.

The ability to exist within open-ended situations is, imaginatively, open to us all: writing a novel, for instance, involves among other burdens, the need to get up every morning, drink a cup of coffee and start imagining the other. What if I were she, what if you were he. And in my own personal background, in my own personal life story and family story, I can't help thinking, very often, that with a slight twist of my genes, or of my parents' circumstances, I could be him or her, I could be a Jewish West Bank settler, I could be an ultra-orthodox extremist, I could be an oriental Jew from a third-world country, I could be anyone. I could be one of my enemies. Imagining this is always a helpful practice. Many years ago, when I was still a child, my very wise grandmother explained to me in very simple words the difference between Jew and Christian – not between Jew and Muslim, but between Jew and Christian: 'You see,' she said, 'Christians believe that the Messiah was here once and he will certainly return one day. The Jews maintain that Messiah is yet to come. Over this,' said my grandmother, 'over this, there has been so much anger, persecution, bloodshed, hatred . . . Why?' She said, 'Why can't everyone simply wait and see? If the Messiah comes, saying, "Hello, it's nice to see you again," the Jews will have to concede. If, on the other hand, the Messiah comes, saying, "How do you do, it is very nice meeting you," the entire

Christian world will have to apologise to the Jews. Between now and then,' said my wise grandmother, 'just live and let live.' She was definitely immune to fanaticism. She knew the secret of living with open-ended situations, with unresolved conflicts, with the otherness of other people.

I began by saying that fanaticism often begins at home. Let me conclude by saying that the antidote can also be found at home, virtually at your fingertips. No man is an island, said John Donne, but I humbly dare to add to this: no man and no woman is an island, but everyone of us is a peninsula, half attached to the mainland, half facing the ocean; half connected to family and friends and culture and tradition and country and nation and sex and language and many other ties. And the other half wants to be left alone to face the ocean. I think we ought to be allowed to remain peninsulas. Every social and political system which turns each of us into a Darwinian island and the rest of humankind into an enemy or a rival is a monster. But at the same time every social and political and ideological system which wants to turn each of us into no more than a molecule of the mainland is also a monstrosity. The condition of peninsula is the proper human condition. That's what we are and that's what we deserve to remain. So, in a sense, in every house, in every family, in every human connection, in every human connection we actually have a relationship between a number of peninsulas and we better remember this before we try to shape each other and turn each other around and make the next person turn our way while he or she actually needs to face the ocean for a while. And this is true of social groups and of cultures and of civilisations and of nations and, yes, of Israelis and Palestinians. Not one of them is an island and not one of them can completely mingle with the other. Those two peninsulas should be related and at the same time left on their own. I know it is an unusual message in these days of violence and anger and revenge and fundamentalism and fanaticism and racism, all of which are loose in the Middle East and elsewhere. A sense of humour, the ability to imagine the other, the capacity to recognise the peninsular quality of everyone of us may be at least a partial defence against the fanatic gene which we all contain.

Postscript to the 'Geneva Accords'

The protests from those who oppose the 'Geneva Accords' are absolutely without foundation. The authors of these agreements know perfectly well that Sharon and his Cabinet are indeed the legitimate government of Israel. They know that their initiative, the fruit of years of negotiation conducted in the greatest secrecy, is no more than an exercise. And that its goal is only to offer to Israeli and Palestinian public opinion a window through which they can see a different landscape: no more car bombs, no more suicide bombers, no more occupations, no more oppression or expropriation, the end to endless war and hate. In their place, we propose a detailed, cautious solution, which does not skirt round any of the fundamental questions. Its central principle is this: we put an end to the occupation, and the Palestinians put an end to their war on Israel. We give up our dream of a Greater Israel, and they give up their dream of a Greater Palestine. We surrender sovereignty of certain parts of the Land of Israel which are dear to our hearts, and the Palestinians do likewise. The problem of the 1948 refugees, which is at the heart of our national security predicament, is to be resolved once and for all, and strictly outside the frontiers of the State of Israel, and with international assistance.

If these agreements are put into action, not a single Palestinian refugee camp, weighed down with its burden of despair, negligence, hate and fanaticism, will remain in the Middle East. In the document we have in our hands, the Palestinians accept, contractually, definitively and irrevocably, that they will not, either now or in the future, claim against Israel.

At the end of the conference, after the signature of the 'Geneva Accords' a representative of the Tanzim declared that perhaps one could now make out on the horizon the end to the hundred-years war between Jews and Palestinians. He added that this would be replaced by a bitter conflict between those on both sides who defend compromise and peace, and those on both sides who are mired in fanaticism. This conflict has already begun to rage. Sharon kicked it off, even before the 'Geneva Accords' were published. And the leaders of Hamas and of the Islamic Jihad rushed to echo him, using exactly the same discourse of hatred.

So what is it that is missing from the 'Geneva Accords'? The 'Geneva Accords' have no teeth. The 'Geneva Accords' are no more than fifty pages of paper. But, on the other hand, if the two sides accept them, tomorrow, or the day after tomorrow, they will discover that the foundations for the peace have already been laid. Right down to the last detail.

If Sharon and Arafat want to use this document as a basis for an agreement, its authors will not claim copyright. And if Sharon works out a better plan, different, more detailed, more nationalistic, and which is accepted by the other camp, what will we do? We will let him do it. We will even congratulate him. And though Sharon is, as everyone knows, a hefty figure of a man, we will carry him shoulder-high, my friends and I.

December 2003

Interview with Amos Oz
(2012)

It has been ten years since you first delivered the lectures in this book. A lot has changed in the past decade, but we don't seem to be much closer to resolving the Israeli–Palestine 'real-estate dispute.' Do you feel gloomier about the prognosis than you did then?

The fanatics on both sides are hard at work trying to turn what I described as a 'real estate dispute' into a Holy War. They have a certain success, both among the Jews and among Arabs. This makes me more pessimistic about the prospect of an imminent Palestinian–Israeli compromise but not less committed: there is no alternative to a two-state solution, Israel next door to Palestine.

Maybe as a result of the lack of momentum, there has been a recent revival of interest in a 'one-state solution,' at least at an academic level. Do you think this could this ever be realisable?

My role model is still the peaceful divorce between the Czechs and the Slovaks when they mutually agreed to dismantle Czechoslovakia into two nation states. The idea of a one-state solution strikes me as a lunatic idea because trying to push the Israelis and the Palestinians into a honeymoon bed together immediately after one hundred and twenty years of bloodshed, hatred and animosity is as absurd as the idea to turn Germany and England into one nation the day World War II ended.

A key element of your argument is that there is a widespread, if reluctant, realisation on

both sides that a two-state solution is inevitable and that it's the leaders who lack the political courage to make it happen. Do you feel that public opinion on both sides has shifted since you first delivered these lectures?

We all hear constantly the bad news from the Middle East but there is some good news too. And the good news is that according to public opinion surveys both in Israel and in Palestine, the majority of the Israelis and the majority of the Palestinians are still ready to accept a two-state solution as an historical compromise. They don't trust each other on anything. They disagree on the partition lines between the two states, they disagree over Jerusalem, settle- ments, security and holy places but they both accept the principle of partition. This in itself is a big step forward if we think of many decades when the Palestinians and the other Arabs refused to recognise the existence of any

Israel anywhere, while the Israelis refused to recognised the existence of a Palestinian people. All of this is over now: each party knows that the other is real, that the other is not going to go away and that the other is going to retain part of the disputed country.

You've spoken elsewhere about the 'corrupt ing' impact of the occupation in terms of embedding relationships of domination and submission, particularly for those undergoing military service. How profound do you think that is? Is it a significant barrier to peace?

The occupation of the West Bank is corrupt ing both the occupier and the occupied. It begets intransigence and racism on the Israeli side, humiliation and vindictiveness on the Palestinian side and reduces mutual confi dence to almost zero. Yet in a strange way, the Israelis and the Palestinians know each other quite intimately and this is a ray of hope in itself.

You addressed *How to Cure a Fanatic* to a European audience, asking in part for a more nuanced media treatment of the conflict. After Gaza and after Lebanon, it's hard not to feel that the European perception of Israel's public policy has actually worsened since you wrote your essay. What are the images of Israel that you feel we're missing most in Europe?

I wish Europe would learn to see the ambiguity of the Israeli–Arab conflict rather than painted in black and white, always asking who are the good guys and who are the bad guys as if it were a Western movie. While Israel is occupying and oppressing the Palestinians on the West Bank, hundreds of millions of zealot Muslims are committed to the destruction of Israel. If you zoom in on Israel and Palestine, then Israel is the ruthless Goliath and Palestine is the heroic David, but if you increase the picture and watch one billion Muslims aiming at the destruction of little Israel, you get a different idea about who is David and who is Goliath.

We have seen enormous changes across the Arab world in the past couple of years. As we begin to see how the consequences of the 'Arab Spring' play out across the region, what do you think the implications are for a resolution of the Israeli–Palestinian conflict?

The term 'Arab Spring' is false and misleading. It was born out of the naive assumption that what happened in the Soviet bloc is going to repeat itself in the Arab world. The dictatorships will collapse like dominos and democracy will prosper. But actually there is no 'Arab Spring'. What is happening in Tunisia is entirely different than what is happening in Egypt and what is happening in Syria is again completely different than what is not yet happening in Saudi Arabia, which might be entirely different than in all the other Arab countries. By and large we see a rise of funda - mentalist militant Islam and it's too early to celebrate the birth of democracy anywhere in the Arab world. For many of the Islamic movements, democracy simply means free elections, one man, one vote . . . *once*.

In particular, how do you think the changes in Egypt may affect the situation?

There has been a cold peace between Israel and Egypt for three decades. I'm afraid it's going to turn now into a frozen peace but I don't think either Israel or Egypt is likely to erase the agreements or to take military actions against each other.

One of the side effects of the 'Arab Spring' has been the popular movements against inequality – the movements of the *indignados*, the occupiers – that have sprung up in many countries. Israel's protests were larger than most, starting with tents being raised in Tel Aviv as a protest against homelessness. What was your immediate reaction to the protests? And is it significant that the protesters' most prominent demands were about housing, privatisation and tuition fees – but not peace?

What happened in the streets of Tel Aviv and other Israeli cities last summer was a powerful demonstration of the strength of the civil society in Israel. Half a million Israelis demonstrated in the streets of Tel Aviv which is the equivalent of roughly five million Brits and there was not a single shattered window, not a single episode of violence. It's beginning to look different this summer because the demonstrators are more frustrated. They demonstrate still about housing and about the cost of living and not about peace because of a certain fatalism, because of a widespread feeling that there is no real partner for peace in the Arab world at this time. In 2006, Israel withdrew unilaterally from the Gaza Strip uprooting 26 Jewish settlements and removing its military, handing every grain of sand back to the Palestinians. We all hoped to get some peace and quiet but, instead, came about 10,000 rockets and missiles on Israeli towns and villages. This is a harsh blow to the Israeli Peace Now Movement who had claimed for many years, 'Let's evacuate the Occupied Territories and we will have peace'. It is very hard for the Peace Movement in Israel to go on advocating 'land for peace' after the Gaza precedent.

It's interesting that in *How to Cure a Fanatic* you touch on the apolitical nature of late

capitalism ('selfish, hedonistic, gadget oriented') as part of the overall problem. Do you think that the lack of social solidarity you have criticised may now be changing?

In some Western countries, including Israel, there are first signs of a certain renewal of a sense of social solidarity. The results of the elections in France may point in this direction but it's too early to tell whether we are actually confronting a universal revival of social solidarity.

One of the recurring themes of your two essays is poor leadership, hampered by short-term political considerations or a lack of courage. Famously, the kinds of new political move-ments we're been seeing have a very different relationship to leadership, rejecting hierarchy. Could this suggest a way of breaking the impasse? Do you think it is fair to say that we